salads

salads

This edition published in 2009

Love Food ® is an imprint of Parragon Books Ltd

Parragon
Queen Street House
4 Queen Street
Bath BA1 1HE, UK

Copyright © Parragon Books Ltd 2008

Love Food ® and the accompanying heart device is a trade mark of Parragon Books Ltd

Cover design by Talking Design
Photography by Günter Beer
Food Styling by Stevan Paul

ISBN 978-1-4075-6968-0

Printed in China

Notes for the reader
• This book uses both metric and imperial measurements. Follow the same units of measurement throughout; do not mix metric and imperial. All spoon measurements are level: teaspoons are assumed to be 5 ml, and tablespoons are assumed to be 15 ml. Unless otherwise stated, milk is assumed to be full fat, eggs and individual vegetables are medium, and pepper is freshly ground black pepper.
• The times given are an approximate guide only. Preparation times differ according to the techniques used by different people and the cooking times may also vary from those given. Optional ingredients, variations or serving suggestions have not been included in the calculations.
• Recipes using raw or very lightly cooked eggs should be avoided by infants, the elderly, pregnant women, convalescents and anyone suffering from an illness. Pregnant and breastfeeding women are advised to avoid eating peanuts and peanut products.

Contents

Salads

Today, salads are one of the ultimate health foods. They can contain an exciting variety of colourful, delicious and satisfying ingredients that provide the nutrients essential for healthy living. We are all being urged to eat more fruit and vegetables every day, and a salad a day can go a long way to helping toward those all important recommendations. With fresh produce from all corners of the globe readily available in supermarkets and farm shops, you can enjoy a variety of salads all year round but, remember, salads are at their most flavoursome and nutritious when made with seasonal produce in its prime.

If you regularly fall back on the old favourite of just tossing a few green leaves with a simple oil-and-vinegar dressing, it's definitely time to think again. It's very easy to mix and match ingredients and the choice has never been greater. And don't make the mistake of thinking all salad ingredients have to be raw, either. Adding small amounts of cooked meat, poultry and seafood to salad leaves and other vegetables gives you a satisfying meal, as the recipes inside this book demonstrate.

Colourful greens
Even with so many ingredients to choose from, salad greens still provide the backbone of many popular salads. Take a look around your supermarket and you'll see leaves in many colours and textures. They also have a variety of flavours, from robust and peppery to sweet, nutty and mild. The greater the variety of leaves you include in your salad, the more interesting it will be, and the more nutrients it will contain. When you select salad leaves, remember that the darker coloured

ones, such as spinach leaves, contain more beta-carotene, which helps fight some forms of cancer and other illnesses. Leafy green vegetables are also excellent sources of fibre.

Keep it fresh

Good salads are only made with good ingredients, and freshness is all-important when buying salad greens. Because of the leaves' high water content, they are very perishable, so buy them as close as possible to serving. Not only will they taste best, but they contain the most nutrients when they are in peak condition, Let your eyes guide you when shopping for salad greens – fresh leaves look fresh. They won't have any leaves tinged with brown, nor will they be wilted or slimy. When you get salad ingredients home, give them a rinse in cold water, then spin them dry or use a tea towel to pat them dry. Never leave them to soak in a sink of cold water because all the water soluble vitamins and minerals will leech out. Use leafy greens as soon as possible, but most will keep for up to four days in a sealed container in the refrigerator. Once you open bags of prepared leaves, however, they should be used within 24 hours. You can prepare salad greens several hours in advance and store in the refrigerator, but do not dress until just before serving, because the acid in most dressings causes the leaves to wilt and become unappetizing.

Classic
Salads

serves 4

280 g/10 oz buffalo
mozzarella, drained and
thinly sliced

8 beef steak tomatoes, sliced

salt and pepper

20 fresh basil leaves

125 ml/4 fl oz extra virgin
olive oil

three-colour salad

Arrange the mozzarella and tomato slices on 4 individual
serving plates and season to taste with salt. Set aside in a cool
place for 30 minutes.

Sprinkle the basil leaves over the salad and drizzle with the olive
oil. Season with pepper and serve immediately.

serves 4

100 g/3¹/₂ oz mixed salad
leaves, such as looseleaf
lettuce, baby spinach and
rocket

500 g/1 lb 2 oz smoked
mozzarella, sliced

for the dressing

140 g/5 oz sun-dried
tomatoes in olive oil (drained
weight), reserving the oil
from the bottle

15 g/¹/₂ oz fresh basil,
coarsely shredded

15 g/¹/₂ oz fresh flat-leaf
parsley, coarsely chopped

1 tbsp capers, rinsed

1 tbsp balsamic vinegar

1 garlic clove, coarsely
chopped

extra olive oil, if necessary

pepper

mozzarella salad with sun-dried tomatoes

Put the sun-dried tomatoes, basil, parsley, capers, vinegar
and garlic in a food processor or blender. Measure the oil from
the sun-dried tomatoes jar and make it up to 150 ml/5 fl oz
with more olive oil if necessary. Add it to the food processor or
blender and process until smooth. Season to taste with pepper.

Divide the salad leaves between 4 individual serving plates. Top
with the slices of mozzarella and spoon the dressing over them.
Serve immediately.

serves 4

225 g/8 oz asparagus spears

1 lamb's lettuce, washed and torn

25 g/1 oz rocket or mizuna leaves

450 g/1 lb ripe tomatoes, sliced

12 black olives, stoned and chopped

1 tbsp toasted pine kernels

for the dressing

1 tsp lemon oil

1 tbsp olive oil

1 tsp wholegrain mustard

2 tbsp balsamic vinegar

sea salt and pepper

asparagus & tomato salad

Steam the asparagus spears for about 8 minutes or until tender. Rinse under cold running water to prevent them cooking any further, then cut into 5-cm/2-inch pieces.

Arrange the lettuce and rocket leaves around a salad platter to form the base of the salad. Place the sliced tomatoes in a circle on top and the asparagus in the centre.

Sprinkle the black olives and pine kernels over the top. Put the lemon oil, olive oil, mustard and vinegar in a screw-top jar and season to taste with sea salt and black pepper. Shake vigorously and drizzle over the salad.

serves 4

2 tbsp olive oil

2 tsp cumin seeds

2 garlic cloves, crushed

2 tsp grated fresh root ginger

300 g/10¹/2 oz split red lentils

700 ml/1¹/4 pints vegetable stock

2 tbsp chopped fresh mint

2 tbsp chopped fresh coriander

2 red onions, thinly sliced

200 g/7 oz baby spinach leaves

1 tsp hazelnut oil

150 g/5¹/2 oz soft goat's cheese

4 tbsp plain yogurt

pepper

warm red lentil salad with goat's cheese

Heat half the olive oil in a large saucepan over a medium heat, add the cumin seeds, garlic and ginger and cook for 2 minutes, stirring constantly.

Stir in the lentils, then add the stock, a ladleful at a time, until it is all absorbed, stirring constantly – this will take about 20 minutes. Remove from the heat and stir in the herbs.

Meanwhile, heat the remaining olive oil in a frying pan over a medium heat, add the onions and cook, stirring frequently, for 10 minutes, or until soft and lightly browned.

Toss the spinach in the hazelnut oil in a bowl, then divide between 4 serving plates.

Mash the goat's cheese with the yogurt in a small bowl and season to taste with pepper.

Divide the lentils between the serving plates and top with the onions and goat's cheese mixture.

serves 4

3 tbsp pine kernels

2 red onions, chopped

4 tbsp olive oil

2 garlic cloves, crushed

3 slices granary bread, cubed

200 g/7 oz mixed salad leaves

250 g/9 oz chestnut mushrooms, sliced

150 g/5 1/2 oz shiitake mushrooms, sliced

150 g/5 1/2 oz oyster mushrooms, torn

for the dressing

1 garlic clove, crushed

2 tbsp red wine vinegar

4 tbsp walnut oil

1 tbsp finely chopped fresh parsley

pepper

mixed mushroom salad

Preheat the oven to 180°C/350°F/Gas Mark 4. Heat a non-stick frying pan over a medium heat, add the pine kernels and cook, turning, until just browned. Tip into a bowl and set aside.

Put the onions and 1 tablespoon of the olive oil into a roasting tin and toss to coat. Roast in the preheated oven for 30 minutes.

Meanwhile, heat 1 tablespoon of the remaining oil with the garlic in the non-stick frying pan over a high heat. Add the bread and cook, turning frequently, for 5 minutes, or until brown and crisp. Remove from the pan and set aside.

Divide the salad leaves between 4 serving plates and add the roasted onions. To make the dressing, whisk the garlic, vinegar and oil together in a small bowl. Stir in the parsley and season to taste with pepper. Drizzle over the salad and onions.

Heat the remaining oil in a frying pan, add the chestnut and shiitake mushrooms and cook for 2–3 minutes, stirring frequently. Add the oyster mushrooms and cook for a further 2–3 minutes. Divide the hot mushroom mixture between the 4 plates. Scatter over the pine kernels and croûtons and serve.

serves 4

2 ripe beef steak tomatoes

100 g/3^1/$_2$ oz mozzarella
cheese

2 avocados

few fresh basil leaves, torn
into pieces

20 black olives

fresh crusty bread, to serve

for the dressing

1 tbsp olive oil

1^1/$_2$ tbsp white wine vinegar

1 tsp coarse grain mustard

salt and pepper

tomato, mozzarella & avocado salad

Using a sharp knife, cut the tomatoes into thick wedges and place in a large serving dish. Drain the mozzarella cheese and roughly tear into pieces. Cut the avocados in half and remove the stones. Cut the flesh into slices, then arrange the mozzarella cheese and avocado with the tomatoes.

Mix the oil, vinegar and mustard together in a small bowl, add salt and pepper to taste, then drizzle over the salad.

Scatter the basil and olives over the top and serve immediately with fresh crusty bread.

serves 4

225 g/8 oz dried conchiglie (pasta shells)

50 g/1¾ oz pine kernels

350 g/12 oz cherry tomatoes, halved

1 red pepper, deseeded and cut into bite-sized chunks

1 red onion, chopped

200 g/7 oz buffalo mozzarella, cut into small pieces

12 black olives, stoned

25 g/1 oz fresh basil leaves

shavings of fresh Parmesan cheese, to garnish

crusty bread, to serve

for the dressing

5 tbsp extra virgin olive oil

2 tbsp balsamic vinegar

1 tbsp chopped fresh basil

salt and pepper

italian salad

Bring a large saucepan of lightly salted water to the boil. Add the pasta and cook over a medium heat for about 10 minutes, or according to the packet instructions. When cooked, the pasta should be tender but still firm to the bite. Drain, rinse under cold running water and drain again. Leave to cool.

While the pasta is cooking, put the pine kernels in a dry frying pan and cook over a low heat for 1–2 minutes until golden brown. Remove from the heat, transfer to a dish and leave to cool.

To make the dressing, put the oil, vinegar and basil into a small bowl. Season with salt and pepper and stir together well. Cover with clingfilm and set to one side.

To assemble the salad, divide the pasta between serving bowls. Add the pine kernels, tomatoes, red pepper, onion, cheese and olives. Scatter over the basil leaves, then drizzle over the dressing. Garnish with fresh Parmesan cheese shavings and serve with crusty bread.

serves 4

200 g/7 oz feta cheese

1/2 head of Webbs lettuce or
1 lettuce such as cos or
escarole, shredded or sliced

4 tomatoes, quartered

1/2 cucumber, sliced

12 Greek black olives, stoned

2 tbsp chopped fresh herbs
such as oregano, flat-leaf
parsley, mint or basil

for the dressing

6 tbsp extra virgin olive oil

2 tbsp fresh lemon juice

1 garlic clove, crushed

pinch of sugar

salt and pepper

greek salad

Make the dressing by whisking together the oil, lemon juice, garlic, sugar, salt and pepper in a small bowl. Set aside. Cut the feta cheese into cubes about 2.5 cm/1 inch square. Put the lettuce, tomatoes and cucumber in a salad bowl. Scatter over the cheese and toss together.

Just before serving, whisk the dressing, pour over the salad leaves and toss together. Scatter over the olives and chopped herbs and serve.

serves 4
85 g/3 oz Puy lentils
450 g/1 lb new potatoes
6 spring onions
1 tbsp olive oil
2 tbsp balsamic vinegar
salt and pepper

warm new potato & lentil salad

Bring a large pan of water to the boil. Rinse the lentils then cook for about 20 minutes or until tender. Drain, rinse and leave to one side.

Meanwhile, steam or boil the potatoes until they are soft right through. Drain and halve.

Trim the base from the spring onions and cut into slices.

Put the lentils, potatoes and spring onions into a serving dish and toss with the olive oil and vinegar. Season with plenty of black pepper and a little salt if required.

serves 4

1 large egg

2 cos lettuces or 3 Little Gem lettuces

6 tbsp olive oil

2 tbsp lemon juice

salt and pepper

8 canned anchovy fillets, drained and roughly chopped

85 g/3 oz fresh Parmesan cheese shavings

garlic croûtons

4 tbsp olive oil

2 garlic cloves

5 slices white bread, crusts removed, cut into 1-cm/ 1/2-inch cubes

caesar salad

Bring a small, heavy-based saucepan of water to the boil.

Meanwhile, make the garlic croûtons. Heat the olive oil in a heavy-based frying pan. Add the garlic and diced bread and cook, stirring and tossing frequently, for 4–5 minutes, or until the bread is crispy and golden all over. Remove from the frying pan with a slotted spoon and drain on kitchen paper.

While the bread is frying, add the egg to the boiling water and cook for 1 minute, then remove from the saucepan and reserve.

Arrange the lettuce leaves in a salad bowl. Mix the olive oil and lemon juice together, then season to taste with salt and pepper. Crack the egg into the dressing and whisk to blend. Pour the dressing over the lettuce leaves, toss well, then add the croûtons and chopped anchovies and toss the salad again. Sprinkle with Parmesan cheese shavings and serve.

Meat & Poultry Salads

serves 4

500 g/1 lb 2 oz red apples, diced

3 tbsp fresh lemon juice

150 ml/5 fl oz mayonnaise

1 head celery

4 shallots, sliced

1 garlic clove, crushed

pepper

90 g/3 oz walnuts, chopped

500 g/1 lb 2 oz lean cooked chicken, cubed

1 cos lettuce

chopped walnuts, to garnish

waldorf chicken salad

Place the apples in a bowl with the lemon juice and 1 tablespoon of mayonnaise. Leave for 40 minutes or until required.

Slice the celery very thinly. Add the celery with the shallots, garlic and walnuts to the apple, mix and then add the remaining mayonnaise and blend thoroughly.

Add the chicken and mix with the other ingredients.

Line a serving dish with the lettuce. Pile the chicken salad into a serving bowl, sprinkle with pepper and garnish with the chopped walnuts.

serves 4

150 g/5$^{1}/_{2}$ oz rocket leaves

2 celery sticks, trimmed and sliced

$^{1}/_{2}$ cucumber, sliced

2 spring onions, trimmed and sliced

2 tbsp chopped fresh parsley

25 g/1 oz walnut pieces

350 g/12 oz boneless roast chicken, sliced

125 g/4$^{1}/_{2}$ oz Stilton cheese, cubed

handful of seedless red grapes, halved (optional)

salt and pepper

for the dressing

2 tbsp olive oil

1 tbsp sherry vinegar

1 tsp Dijon mustard

chicken, cheese & rocket salad

Wash the rocket leaves, pat dry with kitchen paper and put them into a large salad bowl. Add the celery, cucumber, spring onions, parsley and walnuts and mix together well. Transfer onto a large serving platter. Arrange the chicken slices over the salad, then scatter over the cheese. Add the red grapes, if using. Season well with salt and pepper.

To make the dressing, put all the ingredients into a screw-top jar and shake well. Alternatively, put them into a bowl and mix together well. Drizzle the dressing over the salad and serve.

serves 4

400 g/14 oz small new potatoes, scrubbed and halved lengthways

200 g/7 oz baby corn cobs

150 g/5 1/2 oz beansprouts

3 spring onions, trimmed and sliced

4 cooked, skinless chicken breasts, sliced

1 tbsp chopped lemon grass

2 tbsp chopped fresh coriander

salt and pepper

wedges of lime, to garnish

fresh coriander leaves, to garnish

for the dressing

6 tbsp chilli oil or sesame oil

2 tbsp lime juice

thai-style chicken salad

Bring two saucepans of water to the boil. Put the potatoes into one saucepan and cook for 15 minutes until tender. Put the corn cobs into the other saucepan and cook for 5 minutes until tender. Drain the potatoes and corn cobs well and leave to cool.

When the vegetables are cool, transfer them into a large serving dish. Add the beansprouts, spring onions, chicken, lemon grass and coriander and season with salt and pepper.

To make the dressing, put all the ingredients into a screw-top jar and shake well. Alternatively, put them into a bowl and mix together well. Drizzle the dressing over the salad and garnish with lime wedges and coriander leaves. Serve at once.

serves 4

1 litre/1³/4 pints chicken
stock

175 g/6 oz mixed long-grain
and wild rice

2 tbsp sunflower or corn oil

225 g/8 oz skinless, boneless
turkey breast, trimmed of all
visible fat and cut into
thin strips

225 g/8 oz mangetout

115 g/4 oz oyster
mushrooms,
torn into pieces

55 g/2 oz shelled pistachio
nuts, finely chopped

2 tbsp chopped fresh
coriander

salt and pepper

1 tbsp snipped fresh garlic
chives

1 tbsp balsamic vinegar

turkey & rice salad

Reserve 3 tablespoons of the chicken stock and bring the
remainder to the boil in a large saucepan. Add the rice and cook
for 30 minutes, or until tender. Drain and leave to cool slightly.

Meanwhile, heat 1 tablespoon of the oil in a preheated wok
or frying pan. Stir-fry the turkey over a medium heat for
3–4 minutes, or until cooked through. Using a slotted spoon,
transfer the turkey to a dish. Add the mangetout and
mushrooms to the wok and stir-fry for 1 minute. Add the
reserved stock, bring to the boil, then reduce the heat, cover and
simmer for 3–4 minutes. Transfer the vegetables to the dish and
leave to cool slightly.

Thoroughly mix the rice, turkey, mangetout, mushrooms, nuts,
coriander and garlic chives together, then season to taste with
salt and pepper. Drizzle with the remaining sunflower oil and
the vinegar and garnish with fresh garlic chives. Serve warm.

serves 4

350 g/12 oz boneless duckling breasts

2 tbsp plain flour

1 egg

2 tbsp water

2 tbsp sesame seeds

3 tbsp sesame oil

1/2 head Chinese leaves, shredded

3 celery sticks, sliced finely

8 radishes, trimmed and halved

salt and pepper

fresh basil leaves, to garnish

for the dressing

finely grated rind of 1 lime

2 tbsp lime juice

2 tbsp olive oil

1 tbsp light soy sauce

1 tbsp chopped fresh basil

duckling & radish salad

Put each duckling breast between sheets of greaseproof paper or clingfilm. Use a meat mallet or rolling pin to beat them out and flatten them slightly.

Sprinkle the flour onto a large plate and season with salt and pepper. Beat the egg and water together in a shallow bowl, then sprinkle the sesame seeds on to a separate plate.

Dip the duckling breasts first into the seasoned flour, then into the egg mixture and finally into the sesame seeds, to coat the duckling evenly. Heat the sesame oil in a preheated wok or large frying pan.

Fry the duckling breasts over a medium heat for about 8 minutes, turning once. To test whether they are cooked, insert a sharp knife into the thickest part – the juices should run clear. Lift them out and drain on kitchen paper.

To make the dressing for the salad, whisk together the lime rind and juice, olive oil, soy sauce and chopped basil. Season with a little salt and pepper.

Arrange the Chinese leaves, celery and radish on a serving plate. Slice the duckling breasts thinly and place on top of the salad. Drizzle with the dressing and garnish with fresh basil leaves. Serve at once.

serves 4

4 fillet steaks, about 115 g/
4 oz each, fat discarded

2 tbsp red wine vinegar

2 tbsp orange juice

2 tsp ready-made English
mustard

175 g/6 oz new potatoes

115 g/4 oz green beans,
trimmed

175 g/6 oz mixed salad
leaves, such as baby spinach,
rocket and mizuna

1 yellow pepper, peeled,
skinned and
cut into strips

175 g/6 oz cherry tomatoes,
halved

black olives, stoned,
to garnish (optional)

2 tsp extra virgin olive oil

warm beef niçoise

Place the steaks in a shallow dish. Blend the vinegar with
1 tablespoon of orange juice and 1 teaspoon of mustard. Pour
over the steaks, cover and leave in the refrigerator for at least
30 minutes. Turn over halfway through the marinating time.

Meanwhile, place the potatoes in a saucepan and cover with
cold water. Bring to the boil, cover and simmer for 15 minutes,
or until tender when pierced with a fork. Drain and reserve.

Bring a saucepan of water to the boil, add the beans and cook for
5 minutes, or until just tender. Drain, plunge into cold water and
drain again. Arrange the potatoes and beans on top of the salad
leaves together with the yellow pepper, cherry tomatoes and
olives, if using. Blend the remaining orange juice and mustard
with the olive oil and reserve.

Heat a griddle pan until smoking. Drain the steaks and cook for
3–5 minutes on each side or according to personal preference.
Slice the steaks and arrange on top of the salad, then pour over
the dressing and serve.

serves 4

750 g/1 lb 10 oz beef fillet, trimmed of any visible fat

pepper, to taste

2 tsp Worcestershire sauce

3 tbsp olive oil

400 g/14 oz green beans

100 g/3 1/2 oz small pasta, such as orecchiette

2 red onions, finely sliced

1 large head radicchio

50 g/1 3/4 oz green olives, stoned

50 g/1 3/4 oz shelled hazelnuts, whole

for the dressing

1 tsp Dijon mustard

2 tbsp white wine vinegar

5 tbsp olive oil

roast beef salad

Preheat the oven to 220°C/425°F/Gas Mark 7. Rub the beef with pepper to taste and Worcestershire sauce. Heat 2 tablespoons of the oil in a small roasting tin over a high heat, add the beef and sear on all sides. Transfer the dish to the preheated oven and roast for 30 minutes. Remove and leave to cool.

Bring a large saucepan of water to the boil, add the beans and cook for 5 minutes, or until just tender. Remove with a slotted spoon and refresh the beans under cold running water. Drain and put into a large bowl.

Return the bean cooking water to the boil, add the pasta and cook for 11 minutes, or until tender. Drain, return to the saucepan and toss with the remaining oil.

Add the pasta to the beans with the onions, radicchio leaves, olives and hazelnuts, mix gently and transfer to a serving bowl or dish. Arrange some thinly sliced beef on top.

Whisk the dressing ingredients together in a separate bowl, then pour over the salad and serve immediately with extra sliced beef.

serves 4

2 tbsp sunflower oil, plus extra for grilling the lamb

1 tbsp tomato pureé

1/2 tbsp ground cumin

1 tsp lemon juice

1 garlic clove, crushed

pinch of cayenne pepper

salt and pepper

500 g/1 lb 2 oz lamb neck fillets, trimmed with excess fat removed

toasted sesame seeds and chopped fresh parsley, to garnish

for the dressing

2 tbsp fresh lemon juice

1 tsp clear honey

75 g/3 oz Greek yogurt

2 tbsp of finely chopped, fresh herbs

grilled lamb with yogurt & herb dressing

Mix the 2 tablespoons oil, tomato pureé, cumin, lemon juice, garlic, cayenne and salt and pepper to taste together in a non-metallic bowl. Add the lamb fillets and rub all over with the marinade. Cover the bowl and marinate in the fridge for at least 2 hours, but ideally overnight.

Meanwhile, to make the dressing, whisk the lemon juice and honey together until the honey dissolves. Whisk in the yogurt until well blended. Stir in the herbs and add salt and pepper to taste. Cover and chill until required.

Remove the lamb from the fridge 15 minutes before you are ready to cook. Heat the grill to its highest setting and lightly brush the grill rack with oil. Grill the lamb fillet, turning it once, for 10 minutes for medium and 12 minutes for well done. Leave the lamb to cool completely, then cover and chill until required.

Thinly slice the lamb fillets, then divide between 4 plates. Adjust the seasoning in the dressing, if necessary, then spoon over the lamb slices. Sprinkle with toasted sesame seeds and parsley and serve.

serves 4-6

1 small pumpkin, about
1.6 kg/3^1/$_2$ lb, cut in half and
deseeded

2 red onions, cut into wedges

olive oil

100 g/3^1/$_2$ oz green beans,
topped and tailed and cut in
half

600 g/1 lb 5 oz roast pork, any
skin or rind removed and cut
into bite-sized chunks

large handful of fresh rocket
leaves

100 g/3^1/$_2$ oz feta cheese,
drained and crumbled

2 tbsp toasted pine kernels

2 tbsp chopped fresh parsley

salt and pepper

roast pork & pumpkin salad

Preheat the oven to 200°C/400°F/Gas Mark 6. Cut the pumpkin in half, scoop out the seeds and fibres and cut the flesh into wedges about 4 cm/1^1/$_2$ inches wide. Very lightly rub the pumpkin and onion wedges with the olive oil, place in a roasting pan and roast for 25–30 minutes until the pumpkin and onions are tender but holding their shape.

Meanwhile, bring a small pan of salted water to the boil. Add the green beans and blanch for 5 minutes, or until tender. Drain well and cool under cold running water to stop the cooking. Drain well and pat dry.

Remove the pumpkin and onion wedges from the oven as soon as they are tender-crisp and leave to cool completely. When the pumpkin is cool, peel and cut into bite-sized pieces.

To make the vinaigrette, put the oil, vinegar, sugar, mustard and salt and pepper to taste into a screw-top jar and shake until blended.

To assemble the salad, put the pumpkins, onions, beans, pork, rocket, feta, pine kernels and parsley in a large bowl and gently toss together – be careful not to break up the pumpkin. Shake the dressing again, pour over the salad and gently toss. Divide between individual bowls and serve.

serves 4

275 g/9³/₄ oz fresh baby
spinach leaves

2 tbsp olive oil

150 g/5¹/₂ oz pancetta

280 g/10 oz mixed wild
mushrooms, sliced

for the dressing

5 tbsp olive oil

1 tbsp balsamic vinegar

1 tsp Dijon mustard

pinch of sugar

salt and pepper

warm mushroom, spinach & pancetta salad

To make the dressing, place the olive oil, vinegar, mustard, sugar, salt and pepper in a small bowl and whisk together. Rinse the baby spinach under cold running water, then drain and place in a large salad bowl.

Heat the oil in a large frying pan. Add the pancetta and fry for 3 minutes. Add the mushrooms and cook for 3–4 minutes, or until tender.

Pour the dressing into the frying pan and immediately turn the fried mixture and dressing into the bowl with the spinach. Toss until coated with the dressing and serve immediately.

Fish & Seafood Salads

serves 4

2 tuna steaks, about 2 cm/
3/4 inch thick

olive oil

salt and pepper

250 g/9 oz green beans,
topped and tailed

125 ml/4 fl oz vinaigrette or
garlic vinaigrette dressing

2 hearts of lettuce, leaves
separated

3 large hard-boiled eggs,
quartered

2 juicy vine-ripened
tomatoes, cut into wedges

50 g/1³/4 oz anchovy fillets
in oil, drained

55 g/2 oz Niçoise olives,
stoned

salad niçoise

Heat a ridged cast-iron griddle pan over a high heat until you can feel the heat rising from the surface. Brush the tuna steaks with oil, place oiled side down on the hot pan, and chargrill for 2 minutes. Lightly brush the top side of the tuna steaks with more oil. Use a pair of tongs to turn the tuna steaks over, then season to taste with salt and pepper. Continue chargrilling for a further 2 minutes for rare or up to 4 minutes for well done. Leave to cool.

Meanwhile, bring a saucepan of salted water to the boil. Add the beans to the pan and return to the boil, then boil for 3 minutes, or until tender-crisp. Drain the beans and immediately transfer them to a large bowl. Pour over the vinaigrette and stir together, then leave the beans to cool in the dressing.

To serve, line a platter with lettuce leaves. Lift the beans out of the bowl, leaving the excess dressing behind, and pile them in the centre of the platter. Break the tuna into large pieces and arrange it over the beans. Arrange the hard-boiled eggs and tomatoes around the side. Place the anchovy fillets over the salad, then scatter with the olives. Drizzle the remaining dressing in the bowl over everything and serve.

serves 4

200 g/7 oz dried fusilli

1 red pepper, deseeded and quartered

1 red onion, sliced

4 tomatoes, sliced

200 g/7 oz canned tuna in brine, drained and flaked

for the dressing

6 tbsp basil-flavoured oil or extra virgin olive oil

3 tbsp white wine vinegar

1 tbsp lime juice

1 tsp mustard

1 tsp honey

4 tbsp chopped fresh basil, plus extra sprigs to garnish

tuna & herbed fusilli salad

Bring a large saucepan of lightly salted water to the boil. Add the pasta, return to the boil and cook for 8–10 minutes until tender but still firm to the bite.

Meanwhile, put the pepper quarters under a preheated hot grill and cook for 10–12 minutes until the skins begin to blacken. Transfer to a polythene bag, seal and set aside.

Remove the pasta from the heat, drain and set aside to cool. Remove the pepper quarters from the bag and peel off the skins. Slice the pepper into strips.

To make the dressing, put all the dressing ingredients in a large bowl and stir together well. Add the pasta, pepper strips, onion, tomatoes and tuna. Toss together gently, then divide between serving bowls. Garnish with basil sprigs and serve.

serves 4

225 g/8 oz trout fillets

225 g/8 oz white fish fillets
(such as haddock or cod)

300 ml/¹/₂ pint water

1 stalk lemon grass

2 lime leaves

1 large red chilli

1 bunch spring onions,
trimmed and shredded

115 g/4 oz fresh pineapple
flesh, diced

1 small red pepper, deseeded
and diced

1 bunch watercress, washed
and trimmed

fresh snipped chives,
to garnish

for the dressing

1 tbsp sunflower oil

1 tbsp rice wine vinegar

pinch of chilli powder

1 tsp clear honey

salt and pepper

sweet & sour fish salad

Rinse the fish, place in a frying pan and pour over the water.
Bend the lemon grass in half to bruise it and add to the pan with
the lime leaves. Prick the chilli with a fork and add to the pan.
Bring to the boil and simmer for 7–8 minutes. Let cool.

Drain the fish fillet thoroughly, flake the flesh away from the skin
and place in a bowl. Gently stir in the spring onions, pineapple
and pepper.

Arrange the washed watercress on 4 serving plates and spoon
the cooked fish mixture on top.

To make the dressing, mix all the ingredients together, seasoning
well. Spoon over the fish and serve garnished with snipped
chives.

serves 4

50 g/1³/₄ oz wild rocket leaves

1 tbsp chopped fresh flat-leaf parsley

2 spring onions, finely diced

2 large avocados

1 tbsp lemon juice

250 g/9 oz smoked salmon

for the dressing

150 ml/5 fl oz mayonnaise

2 tbsp lime juice

finely grated rind of 1 lime

1 tbsp chopped fresh flat-leaf parsley, plus extra sprigs to garnish

smoked salmon & wild rocket salad

Shred the rocket and arrange in 4 individual glass bowls. Scatter over the chopped parsley and spring onions.

Halve, peel and stone the avocados and cut into thin slices or small chunks. Brush with the lemon juice to prevent discoloration, then divide between the salad bowls. Mix together gently. Cut the smoked salmon into strips and scatter over the top.

Put the mayonnaise in a bowl, then add the lime juice, lime rind and chopped parsley. Mix together well. Spoon some of the mayonnaise dressing on top of each salad and garnish with parsley sprigs.

serves 4

450 g/1 lb new potatoes

4 salmon steaks, about 115 g/4 oz each

1 avocado

juice of 1/2 lemon

55 g/2 oz baby spinach leaves

125 g/41/2 oz mixed small salad leaves, including watercress

12 cherry tomatoes, halved

55 g/2 oz chopped walnuts

for the dressing

3 tbsp unsweetened clear apple juice

1 tsp balsamic vinegar

freshly ground black pepper

salmon & avocado salad

Cut the new potatoes into bite-sized pieces, put into a saucepan and cover with cold water. Bring to the boil, then reduce the heat, cover and simmer for 10–15 minutes, or until just tender. Drain and keep warm.

Meanwhile, preheat the grill to medium. Cook the salmon steaks under the preheated grill for 10–15 minutes, depending on the thickness of the steaks, turning halfway through cooking. Remove from the grill and keep warm.

While the potatoes and salmon are cooking, cut the avocado in half, remove and discard the stone and peel the flesh. Cut the avocado flesh into slices and coat in the lemon juice to prevent it from discolouring.

Toss the spinach leaves and mixed salad leaves together in a large serving bowl until combined, then divide between 4 serving plates. Arrange 6 cherry tomato halves on each plate of salad.

Remove and discard the skin and any bones from the salmon. Flake the salmon and divide between the plates along with the potatoes. Sprinkle the walnuts over the salads.

To make the dressing, mix the apple juice and vinegar together in a small bowl or jug and season well with pepper. Drizzle over the salads and serve immediately.

serves 4

large handful of mixed
lettuce leaves

12 cherry tomatoes, halved

20 black olives, stoned and
halved

6 canned anchovy fillets,
drained and thinly sliced

1 tbsp chopped fresh oregano

wedges of lemon, to garnish

for the dressing

4 tbsp extra virgin olive oil

1 tbsp white wine vinegar

1 tbsp lemon juice

1 tbsp chopped fresh flat-leaf
parsley

salt and pepper

anchovy & olive salad

To make the dressing, put all the ingredients into a small bowl,
season with salt and pepper and stir together well.

To assemble the salad, arrange the lettuce leaves in a serving
dish. Scatter the cherry tomatoes on top, followed by the olives,
anchovies and oregano. Drizzle over the dressing.

Transfer to individual plates and serve.

serves 4

200 g/7 oz brown basmati rice

¹/₂ tsp coriander seeds

2 egg whites, lightly beaten

100 g/3¹/₂ oz unsweetened desiccated coconut

24 raw tiger prawns, peeled

¹/₂ cucumber

4 spring onions, thinly sliced lengthways

1 tsp sesame oil

1 tbsp finely chopped fresh coriander

coconut prawns with cucumber salad

Bring a large saucepan of water to the boil, add the rice and cook for 25 minutes, or until tender. Drain and keep in a colander covered with a clean tea towel to absorb the steam.

Meanwhile, soak 8 wooden skewers in cold water for 30 minutes, then drain. Crush the coriander seeds in a mortar with a pestle. Heat a non-stick frying pan over a medium heat, add the crushed coriander seeds and cook, turning, until they begin to colour. Tip onto a plate and set aside.

Put the egg whites into a shallow bowl and the coconut into a separate bowl. Roll each prawn first in the egg whites, then in the coconut. Thread onto a skewer. Repeat so that each skewer is threaded with 3 coated prawns.

Preheat the grill to high. Using a potato peeler, peel long strips from the cucumber to create ribbons, put into a colander to drain, then toss with the spring onions and oil in a bowl and set aside.

Cook the prawns under the preheated grill for 3–4 minutes on each side, or until slightly browned.

Meanwhile, mix the rice with the toasted coriander seeds and fresh coriander and divide this and the cucumber salad between bowls. Serve with the hot prawn skewers.

serves 4

350 g/12 oz fresh crabmeat

5 tbsp mayonnaise

50 ml/2 fl oz natural yogurt

4 tsp extra virgin olive oil

4 tsp lime juice

1 spring onion, finely chopped

4 tsp finely chopped fresh parsley

pinch of cayenne pepper

1 cantaloupe melon

2 radicchio heads, separated into leaves

fresh parsley sprigs, to garnish

cantaloupe & crab salad

Place the crabmeat in a large bowl and pick over it very carefully to remove any remaining shell or cartilage, but try not to break the meat up.

Place the mayonnaise, yogurt, olive oil, lime juice, spring onion, chopped fresh parsley and cayenne pepper into a separate bowl and mix until thoroughly blended. Fold in the crabmeat.

Cut the melon in half and remove and discard the seeds. Slice into wedges, then cut off the rind with a sharp knife.

Arrange the melon wedges and radicchio leaves in 4 serving bowls, then arrange the crabmeat mixture on top. Garnish with a few sprigs of fresh parsley and serve.

serves 2

2 raw lobster tails

radicchio leaves

fresh dill sprigs, to garnish

for the mayonnaise

1 large lemon

1 large egg yolk

1/2 tsp Dijon mustard

150 ml/5 fl oz olive oil

salt and pepper

1 tbsp chopped fresh dill

lobster salad

To make the lemon-dill mayonnaise, finely grate half the lemon rind and squeeze the juice. Beat the egg yolk in a small bowl, then beat in the mustard and 1 teaspoon of the lemon juice.

Using a balloon whisk or electric mixer, beat the oil into the egg yolk mixture, drop by drop, until a thick mayonnaise forms. Stir in the lemon rind and 1 tablespoon of the remaining lemon juice.

Season the mayonnaise to taste with salt and pepper and add more lemon juice if desired. Stir in the dill, cover and chill in the refrigerator until required.

Bring a large saucepan of lightly salted water to the boil. Add the lobster tails, return to the boil and cook for 6 minutes, or until the flesh is opaque and the shells are red. Drain immediately and set aside to cool.

Remove the lobster flesh from the shells and cut into bite-sized pieces. Arrange the radicchio leaves on individual plates and top with the lobster flesh. Place a spoonful of the lemon-dill mayonnaise on the side. Garnish with dill sprigs and serve.

serves 4

250 g/9 oz live mussels

350 g/12 oz live scallops, shucked and cleaned

250 g/9 oz prepared squid, cut into rings and tentacles

1 red onion, halved and finely sliced

chopped parsley and lemon wedges, to serve

for the dressing

4 tbsp extra virgin olive oil

2 tbsp white wine vinegar

1 tbsp lemon juice

1 garlic clove, finely chopped

1 tbsp chopped fresh flat-leaf parsley

salt and pepper

seafood salad

Clean the mussels by scrubbing or scraping the shells and pulling out any beards that are attached to them. Discard any with broken shells or any that refuse to close when tapped. Put the mussels in a colander and rinse well under cold running water. Put them in a large saucepan with a little water and cook, covered, over a high heat, shaking the saucepan occasionally, for 3–4 minutes, or until the mussels have opened. Discard any mussels that remain closed. Strain the mussels, reserving the cooking liquid. Refresh the mussels under cold running water, drain and set aside.

Return the reserved cooking liquid to the saucepan and bring to the boil, add the scallops and squid and cook for 3 minutes. Remove from the heat and drain. Refresh under cold running water and drain again. Remove the mussels from their shells. Put them in a bowl with the scallops and squid and leave to cool. Cover with clingfilm and chill in the refrigerator for 45 minutes.

Divide the seafood between 4 serving plates and top with the onion. Combine all the dressing ingredients in a small bowl, then drizzle over the salad. Garnish with chopped parsley and lemon wedges to serve.

Healthy Salads

serves 4

225 g/8 oz wild rice

850 ml/1¹/2 pints water

1 each red, yellow and orange peppers, skinned, deseeded and thinly sliced

¹/2 cucumber, halved lengthways and sliced

1 orange, peeled, pith removed and cubed

3 ripe tomatoes, cut into chunks

1 red onion, chopped very finely

generous handful of chopped flat-leaf parsley

for the dressing

1 clove garlic, crushed

1 tbsp balsamic vinegar

sea salt and black pepper

2 tbsp extra virgin olive oil

wild rice salad with cucumber & orange

Put the wild rice and water into a large pan and bring to the boil. Stir, cover and simmer for about 40 minutes or until the rice is al dente (firm to the bite). Uncover the rice for the last few minutes of cooking to allow any excess water to evaporate.

To make the dressing, put the crushed garlic, vinegar, olive oil and seasoning into a screw-top jar and shake vigorously. Add extra vinegar, oil or seasoning as required.

Drain the rice and turn into a large bowl. Pour over the dressing and mix in. Then mix in the chopped peppers, cucumber, orange, tomatoes, red onion and flat-leaf parsley and serve.

serves 4

115 g/4 oz beansprouts,
washed and dried

small bunch seedless black
and green grapes, halved

12 unsulphured dried
apricots, halved

25 g/1 oz blanched almonds,
halved

black pepper

for the dressing

1 tbsp walnut oil

1 tsp sesame oil

2 tsp balsamic vinegar

beansprout, apricot & almond salad

Place the beansprouts in the bottom of a large salad bowl and sprinkle the grapes and apricots on top.

Place the oils and vinegar in a screw-top jar and shake vigorously to mix. Pour over the salad.

Scatter over the almonds and season with freshly ground black pepper.

serves 4

175 g/6 oz quinoa

600 ml/1 pint water

10 vine-ripened cherry tomatoes, halved

7.5-cm/3-inch piece cucumber, diced

3 spring onions, finely chopped

juice of 1/2 lemon

2 tbsp extra virgin olive oil

4 tbsp chopped fresh mint

4 tbsp chopped fresh coriander

4 tbsp chopped fresh parsley

salt and pepper

tabbouleh

Put the quinoa into a medium-sized saucepan and cover with the water. Bring to the boil, then reduce the heat, cover and simmer over a low heat for 15 minutes. Drain if necessary.

Leave the quinoa to cool slightly before combining with the remaining ingredients in a salad bowl. Adjust the seasoning, if necessary, before serving.

serves 4

2 courgettes, cut into batons

100 g/3¹/₂ oz green beans, cut into thirds

1 green pepper, deseeded and cut into strips

2 celery sticks, sliced

1 bunch of watercress

for the dressing

200 ml/7 fl oz natural yogurt

1 garlic clove, crushed

2 tbsp chopped fresh mint

pepper

courgette & mint salad

Cook the courgette batons and beans in a saucepan of lightly salted water for 7–8 minutes. Drain, rinse under cold running water and drain again. Leave to cool completely.

Mix the courgettes and beans with the green pepper strips, celery and watercress in a large serving bowl.

To make the dressing, combine the yogurt, garlic and mint in a small bowl. Season to taste with pepper.

Spoon the dressing onto the salad and serve immediately.

serves 4-6

175 g/6 oz mixed salad leaves, such as spinach, rocket and curly endive

1 red onion

85 g/3 oz radishes

175 g/6 oz cherry tomatoes

115 g/4 oz cooked beetroot

280 g/10 oz canned cannellini beans, drained and rinsed

200 g/7 oz canned red kidney beans, drained and rinsed

300 g/10^{1}/$_{2}$ oz canned flageolet beans, drained and rinsed

40 g/1^{1}/$_{2}$ oz dried cranberries

55 g/2 oz roasted cashew nuts

225 g/8 oz feta cheese (drained weight), crumbled

three bean salad

Arrange the salad leaves in a salad bowl and reserve.

Thinly slice the onion, then cut in half to form half moons and put into a bowl.

Thinly slice the radishes, cut the tomatoes in half and peel the beetroot, if necessary, and dice. Add to the onion with the remaining ingredients, except the nuts and cheese.

Put all the ingredients for the dressing into a screw-top jar and shake until blended. Pour over the bean mixture, toss lightly, then spoon on top of the salad leaves.

Scatter over the nuts and cheese and serve immediately.

serves 2

200 g/7 oz buckwheat noodles

250 g/9 oz firm smoked tofu (drained weight)

200 g/7 oz white cabbage, finely shredded

250 g/9 oz carrots, finely shredded

3 spring onions, diagonally sliced

1 fresh red chilli, deseeded and finely sliced into rounds

2 tbsp sesame seeds, lightly toasted

for the dressing

1 tsp grated fresh root ginger

1 garlic clove, crushed

175 g/6 oz silken tofu

buckwheat noodle salad with smoked tofu

Cook the noodles in a large saucepan of lightly salted boiling water according to the packet instructions. Drain and refresh under cold running water.

To make the dressing, blend the ginger, garlic, silken tofu, soy sauce, oil and water together in a small bowl until smooth and creamy. Season to taste with salt.

Place the smoked tofu in a steamer. Steam for 5 minutes, then cut into thin slices.

Meanwhile, put the cabbage, carrots, spring onions and chilli into a bowl and toss to mix. To serve, arrange the noodles on serving plates and top with the carrot salad and slices of tofu. Spoon over the dressing and sprinkle with sesame seeds.

serves 4

large handful of radicchio
leaves

large handful of rocket leaves

1 small galia melon

2 ripe avocados

1 tbsp lemon juice

200 g/7 oz fontina cheese,
cut into bite-sized pieces

for the dressing

5 tbsp lemon-flavoured or
extra virgin olive oil

1 tbsp white wine vinegar

1 tbsp lemon juice

1 tbsp chopped fresh parsley

avocado salad

To make the dressing, mix together the oil, vinegar, lemon juice
and parsley in a small bowl.

Arrange the radicchio and rocket on serving plates. Halve and
deseed the melon, then cut the flesh from the skin. Discard the
skin. Slice the melon flesh and arrange it over the salad leaves.

Cut the avocados in half and remove and discard the stones and
skin. Slice the flesh and brush with lemon juice. Arrange the
slices over the melon, then scatter over the cheese. Drizzle over
the dressing, garnish with chopped fresh parsley and serve.

serves 4

175 g/6 oz dried chickpeas or
400 g/14 oz canned, drained
and rinsed

225 g/8 oz ripe tomatoes,
roughly chopped

1 red onion, thinly sliced

handful of fresh basil leaves,
torn

1 cos lettuce, torn

crusty bread, to serve

for the dressing

1 green chilli, deseeded and
finely chopped

1 clove garlic, crushed

juice and zest of 2 lemons

2 tbsp olive oil

1 tbsp water

black pepper

chickpea & tomato salad

If using dried chickpeas, soak overnight then boil for at least 30 minutes until soft. Leave to cool.

Put the chilli, garlic, lemon juice, olive oil, water and black pepper in a screw-top jar and shake vigorously. Taste and add more lemon juice or oil if necessary.

Add the tomatoes, onion and basil to the chickpeas and mix gently. Pour over the dressing and mix again. Arrange on a bed of lettuce and serve with crusty bread.

serves 4

85 g/3 oz cucumber, cut into batons

6 spring onions, halved

2 tomatoes, deseeded and cut into 8 wedges

1 yellow pepper, deseeded and cut into strips

2 celery sticks, cut into strips

4 radishes, quartered

85 g/3 oz rocket

1 tbsp chopped fresh mint, to garnish (optional)

for the dressing

2 tbsp lemon juice

1 garlic clove, crushed

150 ml/5 fl oz natural yogurt

2 tbsp olive oil

salt and pepper

salad with garlic dressing

To make the salad, gently mix the cucumber batons, spring onions, tomato wedges, yellow pepper strips, celery, radishes and rocket in a large serving bowl.

To make the dressing, stir the lemon juice, garlic, natural yogurt and olive oil together in a small bowl until thoroughly combined. Season with salt and pepper to taste.

Spoon the dressing over the salad and toss to mix. Sprinkle the salad with chopped mint (if using) and serve.

serves 4

1 sweet potato

4 baby carrots, halved

4 tomatoes

4 celery sticks, chopped

225 g/8 oz canned borlotti beans, drained and rinsed

115 g/4 oz mixed salad leaves, such as curly endive, rocket, radicchio and looseleaf lettuce

1 tbsp sultanas

4 spring onions, sliced diagonally

for the dressing

2 tbsp lemon juice

1 garlic clove, crushed

150 ml/5 fl oz natural yogurt

2 tbsp olive oil

sweet potato & bean salad

Peel and dice the sweet potato. Bring a saucepan of water to the boil over a medium heat. Add the sweet potato and cook for 10 minutes, or until tender. Drain, transfer to a bowl and reserve until required.

Cook the carrots in a separate saucepan of boiling water for 1 minute. Drain thoroughly and add to the sweet potato. Cut the tops off the tomatoes and scoop out the seeds. Chop the flesh and add to the bowl with the celery and beans. Mix well.

Line a large serving bowl with the mixed salad leaves. Spoon the sweet potato and bean mixture on top, then sprinkle with the sultanas and spring onions.

Put all the dressing ingredients in a screw-top jar, with salt and pepper to taste, screw on the lid and shake until well blended. Pour over the salad and serve.